MAGNIFICENT OASIS

AT
DEATH VALLEY

David & Gayle Woodruff

David & Gayle Woodruff

Death Valley and Vicinity
Region of Mystery and Scenic Grandeur

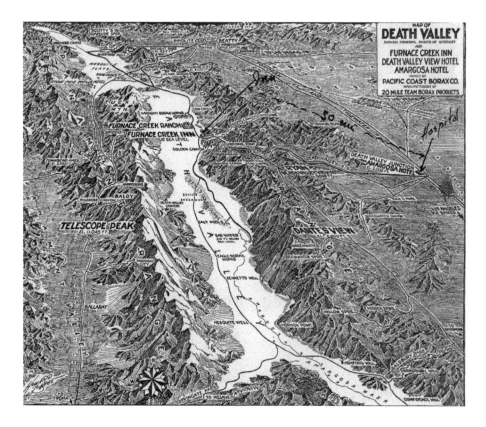

Copyright © 2019
David & Gayle Woodruff
All Rights Reserved
ISBN- 978-0-578-43165-9

El Camino Sierra Publishing
elcaminosierra395@gmail.com

ACKNOWLEDGMENTS

One of our greatest passions in life is Death Valley National Park, its stunning scenery and its human and natural history. We feel so fortunate to have had the opportunity to have been residents of this spectacular piece of desert real estate for over 18 years, while we were employed at the Oasis at Death Valley Resort...formerly Furnace Creek Resort. Our many years of association with this historic property spawned a deep interest in this one of kind jewel. We felt privileged to have followed in the foot-steps of the legions of dedicated staff members who created the Resort's storied history with their exceptional level of hospitality and service.

Over our time at this wonderful property we had the good fortune to meet and come to know hundreds if not thousands of incredible co-workers, and guests...some of whom were former employees of the Resort from several years ago. Many of these remarkable people contributed to our knowledge of Death Valley and the Oasis Resort that we now share with our readers here in this book...and we are so very grateful to you all.

We also express special thanks to a few people and organizations in particular, who provided volumes of little and lesser known bits of the Resort's history, allowing us to put together something we hope is not only highly entertaining and informative, but accurate as well. In particular; Rio Tinto Borax (formerly U.S. Borax and before that, Pacific Coast Borax), Mike Reynolds and the exceptional staff of Death Valley National Park, Xanterra Travel Collection, Union Pacific Railroad, Eastern California Museum, Lasley Biven, Christine Watts and our dear friend and former co-worker Alex Cabana. And a very special thank you to Naiya Luna-Warren of Independence, California, our editing assistant.

The Inn at the Oasis at Death Valley

CONTENTS

INTRODUCTION

As we travel the road of life, we find it will not only take us to unexpected places, but it will also take us to places we already know. In 2018, like a butterfly, the Oasis at Death Valley transformed itself into a beautiful new life that will forever be tied to its essential and historic past.

For many people, the words Furnace Creek Resort have been synonymous with Death Valley National Park. The history of both is deep and rich, and intricately intertwined. Though Death Valley was well known for many years before the arrival of tourists, it has been only since the traveling public has made its way into this immeasurable expanse of portentous and arid wilderness, that it's many secrets and mysteries have come to be known.

The Resort encompasses two different properties; the Inn at the Oasis at Death Valley and the Ranch at the Oasis at Death Valley. Though vastly different, the two properties have always been intimately tied, with their respective and individual services always complimenting each other. The water for the Resorts comes from springs located near the Inn. The golf course at the Ranch was first built to accommodate the guests at the Inn. An airport built to handle commercial air travel to Death Valley was built at the Ranch. Each property has done much to help with the success of the other.

John Steinbeck wrote, "People don't take trips, trips take people." For the first visitors who came to Death Valley, taking a trip meant traveling on appalling roads and trails, and staying in the hovels and dugouts of desert prospectors. Just to get there from Southern California could take more than two full days of travel in the early 1900s. The only road that existed for much of the way was the route taken by the famed Twenty Mule Teams to haul their precious cargo to market. A trip to Death Valley was an experience in and of itself.

Without decent accommodations, tourist travel to Death Valley was pretty light for the first few years of the 20th century. The dime store novels and early travel publications were still portraying Death Valley as a spot only the fearless should visit.

But in 1927, the opening of the Inn began to change all that. Visitors could now come to this land of dread and fear and enjoy it in comfort and elegance that rivaled the offerings of the finest hotels in Europe. Fearsome and mysterious Death Valley was tamed. The opening of the

Inn truly put Death Valley on the map as a place that people could now safely visit. And visit they did. Five thousand people are estimated to have visited this remote and far off land in the first year of the Inn's opening.

The history of the Oasis at Death Valley is also an excellent example of entrepreneurship and free enterprise at their very best. Prior to constructing the Inn, the Pacific Coast Borax Company had no experience whatsoever in the hospitality business. To attempt their first venture into this field in a location whose appeal to tourism seemed rather sketchy at best, was risk taking at its highest level. What did a business famous for making laundry soaps know about tourism? How could a place named Death Valley be turned into a destination that people would actually want to come and vacation?

Important to remember is that when the Inn opened in 1927, Death Valley was not a National Park or a National Monument. It had no protected federal status whatsoever. It was simply a large expanse of raw California and Nevada desert with a foreboding sounding name. It was best known for borax mining and for gold seekers who nearly lost their lives here in 1849.

Most roads in Death Valley at that time were mere trails built for mining equipment. No designated scenic spots for tourists had yet been developed. All the promotion and development of tourism in Death Valley was going to fall squarely on the Borax Company without any assistance from the federal or state government.

By the time Death Valley was designated a National Monument in 1933, 10,000 people a year were visiting. The Inn had already been expanded four times and the Ranch was renting rooms as well. Pacific Coast Borax Company had taken a bold gamble, and it had paid off.

Today, over 90 years after the Inn first opened, Death Valley enjoys almost one and a half million visitors a year. This largest of National Parks outside of Alaska, enjoys preeminence as a "must see" treasure for Americans and international visitors alike. The hotels at the Oasis at Death Valley are more popular than ever and the importance of its rich and historic past forms the foundation of the exceptional hospitality that is their hallmark today.

Would You Enjoy a Trip to Hell?

Probably you would not. At least we will suppose so. Even if you would enjoy it there is no hurry about starting. If you are going you will do so sometime without having to plan ahead of time.

You Might Enjoy a Trip to Death Valley, Now!

It has all the advantages of hell without the inconveniences. It is a wonderful country with all the weird mysticism of Dante's Inferno, marvelous scenery, strange romanticism, fabulous wealth and absolute novelty. If you would enjoy a change from ordinary city life and fashionable summer resort outings you would find it here. You would see and learn of things of which you have never dreamed. *An automobile trip through hell* would certainly be a novelty. Such an excursion through Death Valley would be no less wonderful and much more comfortable. You may have this. If you are interested write to

The Mining Advertising Agency, Greenwater, Cal.

 *One*

The Miracle of Borax

A history of the Oasis at Death Valley/Furnace Creek Resort could not be written without including the history of borax mining in Death Valley. Pacific Coast Borax Company had been in the Death Valley area for over 40 years when they built the Furnace Creek Inn. The mining of borax brought large profits to the Borax Company and helped support their move to build their hotels and develop tourism.

In 1882, Aaron and Rosie Winters were living a life of destitution at Ash Meadows near Death Valley. One evening, they learned from a passing prospector that the mineral borax was turning nice profits for its investors at nearby mines in Nevada. Aaron listened intently as he was told how borax was often found on dry lakebeds and that the way to test for borax was to take sulfuric acid and alcohol, mix it with the mineral and when lit with a match, would burn with a green flame if it were borax. When the prospector left, the Winters made an immediate trip to the dry lake bed 30 miles to their west known as Death Valley. They brought with them the alcohol and sulfuric acid they would need and headed straight out onto the valley floor. They waited until the darkness of night, gathered some of the white powder from the dry lakebed, added the acid and alcohol and lit the match. Aaron shouted, "she burns green Rosie, by God we're rich."

In the Furnace Creek vicinity lies a vast expanse of borax on Death Valley's floor. Its acicular crystals often form into what looks like beautiful cotton ball tufts. The Winters quickly filed claims on 4,000 acres of the valuable mineral and just as quickly sold their claims to investor William T. Coleman of San Francisco.

The amount of borax on the floor of Death Valley was almost unlimited. There was no doubt there was enough to meet the world's demands for many years. However, Death Valley's remote location and associated transportation costs would make it difficult to get the valuable mineral to market at a cost that would allow Coleman to make a profit.

A plant was constructed to refine the raw borax into a purer form to haul out of Death Valley. The plant was named Harmony Borax Works after one of Coleman's daughters. Up to 40 laborers worked here and lived at the nearby oasis two miles south. The raw borax was brought in wheeled carts from two miles distant, offloaded and then refined by boiling it in vats of water. The refined product would crystallize onto metal rods and this purified product would then be hauled to Wilmington, California for further processing.

Harmony Borax Works located 2 miles north of the Ranch

It was 165 miles from Death Valley to the nearest railroad station where the refined borax could be transported economically to southern California. And these 165 miles were across some of the most difficult terrain to be found anywhere. Steep passes, swampy mud bogs, knife edged salt fields, and a lack of water were just some of the obstacles that had to be faced.

Coleman instructed his foreman J.W. Perry to devise a method to get the borax out of Death Valley and to the railroad at an affordable cost. Perry had formerly been a druggist in San Francisco and knew little about the freighting business. But he took on Coleman's task and engineered some of the most efficient freight wagons ever designed.

The 20-Mule Team Wagons hauled borax out of Death Valley for almost five years. These massive freight wagons would haul over 10 tons of ore, and together with the 500-gallon water tank, would weigh over 72,000 pounds when fully loaded. The 20-Mule Teams were usually composed of 18 mules and two horses. The horses, being bigger and stronger, would be placed at the wagon's tongue to provide better steering. The animals were trained to jump over the drag line on sharp turns, with the front mules pulling at almost 90 degrees to the wagon to avoid tipping them over. Two men were required to operate the teams, a teamster and a swamper. The teamster would ride in the front wagon, often standing while guiding the mules. The swamper would usually walk, throwing rocks at the mules to encourage them along. The 165-mile trip took 10 days to complete. Five sets of these wagons were built and not once did they suffer a serious break down during their five years of use.

The borax operation in Death Valley would employ upwards of 60 to 70 men at its peak. To house their workers and to provide feed for the mules, the Borax Company took advantage of the water from the natural springs located just a few miles to the southeast. A ranch was developed to house the workers and grow alfalfa for the animals. It was named

Greenland Ranch.

In addition to borax, Coleman invested heavily in a number of other ventures. He soon found himself overextended and deeply in debt. He was forced to sell his Death Valley borax operations to his competitor and Oakland, California businessman, Frances Marion Smith, who soon came to become known as the Borax King.

Francis M. Smith-the Borax King

Smith's Pacific Coast Borax Company mined borax in the Death Valley area off and on for the next 39 years. Though the use of the 20-Mule Teams ended in 1887, a brilliant executive in the Borax Company's marketing department named Stephen Mather, incorporated the legendary teams into their marketing campaign and their product was sold under the 20-Mule Team label. This began one of the most successful advertising campaigns of all time. People across the country became familiar with Death Valley through the story told on the box of laundry soap. In 1892, the Borax Company hired columnist John Spears to produce a book, *Illustrated Sketches of Death Valley*, where a number of interesting Death Valley facts as well as far flung fantasies were published. The American public was becoming well familiar with this remote and mysterious place. In lore and in fact, Death Valley soon became an image of the mind and a curiosity to visit.

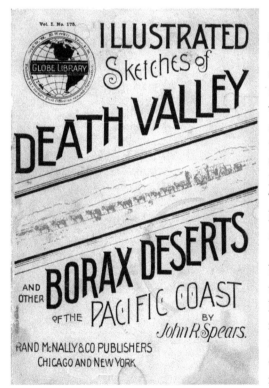

The use of borax skyrocketed, and the Borax Company did everything it could to meet the demand for its product. A railroad was built nearly to the heart of Death Valley to haul out the huge quantities the Borax Company was now mining. Known as the Tonopah and Tidewater, the railroad also hauled other types of ore from nearby mines.

The Borax Company even built the small town of Ryan to accommodate the hundreds of miners it was now employing and their families. Fresh meat from cattle and pigs raised at nearby Greenland Ranch along with locally grown produce kept the miners fed. Weekly motion pictures, a church and school house added to the sense of refinement. It seemed borax had started to bring civilization to the once feared Death Valley.

The borax mining camp at Ryan supported over 200 miners at its peak, and included a school and a church

 # *TWO*

An Epitaph of Infamy

Interest in Death Valley grew for reasons other than just borax. Manufacturers of everything from automobiles to cigars began to market the stoutness and durability of their product because it had endured some form of Death Valley trial. Newspaper editors poked fun at the notion that anyone would be interested in visiting the "foreboding valley." The idea of people coming to Death Valley to relax, enjoy and have a good time, in a place so identified with fear and dread, seemed improbable at the very least.

Death Valley's reputation as a place to fear was not helped when on July 10, 1913, during a particularly blistering heat wave, Oscar Denton, the caretaker at Greenland Ranch officially recorded 134°F at the U.S. Weather Bureau's Death Valley weather station. This became and still is the world's record for hottest air temperature ever recorded.

The U.S. Weather Bureau's station at Greenland Ranch circa 1913

One of the first widely distributed publications about Death Valley was *Through Death Valley in a Dodge Brothers Motor Car* which touted the exploits of the Dodge brother's automobile in "the most strenuous trip ever recorded in the annals of motoring through the most fearsome spot in America at 141°F."

TO win through the most dreaded region in the United States, overcoming with a motor car vast stretches of desert waste, miles of shifting sand dunes, mountain ranges over a mile high, then across Death Valley below sea level in a temperature of 144°, forms a tale so thrilling that every motorist will be interested in reading of the most strenuous trip ever recorded in the annals of motoring.

Away down in the southwest corner of the United States there are two regions so absolutely different in their physical make-up as to be a cause of wonderment even to those who are thoroughly familiar with both.

Everyone thinks of Southern California as the garden spot of America. Not a thought is ever given to that desert land lying just to the east of the Sierra Nevada Mountains, which holds in its midst one of the most dreaded regions on earth. In fact, it is scarcely believable that within two hundred miles of Los Angeles there is in reality the valley of "Il Mort" that has been the cause of more deaths by thirst and starvation than any other equal area on the earth's surface.

Such, however, is the irony of fate to which many a man has been subjected in striving, from inland empires, to reach that promised land between the mountains and the sea. Tales there are without number of those who have attempted to cross Death Valley in prospecting and exploring, who have suffered most horrible deaths, but rarely has the attempt been made to negotiate this arid region with a motor car.

The Dodge brother's "Through Death Valley…"

In 1923, famed movie director Eric Von Stroheim came to Death Valley during the hottest part of summer in an attempt to draw real emotion from his cast while he filmed the closing scenes of the MGM classic *Greed*. Studio executives and their insurance company tried to dissuade him warning of the perils of "poison water, treacherous quicksand" and the "death dealing gas and poison fumes."

Even western novelist Zane Grey took a shot when he wrote in Harpers Magazine of his 1918 visit to Death Valley. "It was an ashen gray through a leaden haze...an abyss of ashes. Iron walled and sun blasted...as hateful and horrible as the portal of hell." Grey went on, "Death Valley will never be popular with men and is fatal to women."

It seemed for a time, nothing was worth buying unless it had passed the rigorous test of surviving the worst of what Death Valley could offer. Advertisers shamelessly promoted their products as being the best and most durable because they had "survived" Death Valley.

Western novelist Zane Grey visited Death Valley in the spring of 1918

Finally, the Automobile Club of Southern California came to the Valley's defense when it proclaimed that car dealers and advertisers were making Death Valley, "the most maligned natural attraction in America, trying to make the public think their cars are wonders because they penetrate the awful mysteries of Death Valley."

Advertisers were not the only ones that tarnished Death Valley's reputation. The first two decades of the 20th century saw hundreds if not thousands of prospectors roaming the mountains and canyons searching for precious minerals. The newspapers dutifully reported the many that met a deadly fate at the hands of a sometimes harsh and unforgiving Death Valley climate.

Though borax had not been taken out of Death Valley by mules for 16 years, Borax's marketing department coined the name "20-Mule Team Borax" as the way to promote their wondrous product. Pacific Coast Borax resurrected two of the old sets of wagons, trained new teams of mules to pull them and sent them on a promotional tour including an appearance at the 1904, St. Louis World Expo. The great 20-Mule Teams were hugely popular and people flocked to see them. A motion picture company produced a short film about them creating even more publicity. The team's appearance in St. Louis was so popular that the Borax Company sent them on a tour of cities throughout the East Coast, drawing huge crowds as salesmen handed out free samples of borax. Thanks to this masterful marketing campaign, the demand for borax by American households continued to skyrocket and public opinion about the mysterious and dreadful valley began to soften.

The appearance of the 20-Mule Team Wagons at the 1904
St. Louis Exhibition drew huge crowds

About the same time, the discovery of gold at nearby Rhyolite brought a flood of positive publicity and attention to Death Valley. Rhyolite quickly became one of the most successful boom towns in the west boasting a population of over 5,000 inhabitants, with piped water and electric lights. Hundreds of prospectors combed every canyon, mountain and valley of Death Valley during this time, hoping to strike it rich. Dozens of other mining camps came and went in Death Valley and the surrounding area over the next few decades as prospectors and miners flowed with the cycle of boom and bust.

The gold camp of Rhyolite

During the first two decades of the 20th century, Death Valley received a great deal of publicity from advertisers, novelists and promoters. The stories, both true and fiction, brought more and more focus on this remote and isolated land. America's love affair with the automobile was also taking hold in the American psyche and despite the near complete absence of decent roads, a number of people were finding their way to this land of mystery in their horseless carriages. More and more people were seeing for themselves that this vast expanse of arid land was filled with a beauty unparalleled and not seen in most desert landscapes. And while other scenic areas were often cold and gloomy for a good part of the year with their snowy scenes or fog shrouded coastlines, the sun shined brightly in Death Valley during the coldest and darkest reaches of winter. Maybe, just maybe, Death Valley might indeed be…a nice place to visit.

During the first few years of the 20th century, prospectors combed
every inch of Death Valley in search of gold and silver

THREE

A Bold Endeavour

"Some people will dream big dreams while others wake up and do them."-John Blytheway. By the mid-1920s, the Pacific Coast Borax Company had become one of the most successful corporations in America. The success of their product had surpassed even their own ambitious forecasts. However, within the Borax Company's hierarchy, there were those dreaming of exploring a completely new revenue stream.

"Simply start you wash and let Borax finish it"

The widespread introduction of borax and its powerful cleaning properties to the home-makers of America brought unprecedented growth to Pacific Coast Borax Company. No longer was washday quite the dreaded chore it had been. As the advertisement (previous page) states, "Simply start your wash and let Borax finish it." The Borax Company not only mined the valuable mineral, it processed and marketed it as well. The profit the company was reaping made it one of the corporate powerhouses of the 1920s. The success the Borax Company enjoyed gave it the appearance of infallibility to investors and the public alike.

The introduction of borax products changed the lives of millions

Francis Marion Smith had founded Pacific Coast Borax Company after purchasing William Coleman's holdings. Smith, like Coleman, took the profits from his borax mining and invested in a number of other endeavors. Smith's investments became so numerous he soon found himself overextended. Finding a need for cash, Smith created one of the first multi-national companies when he combined with Borax Consolidated, LTD of England in a $12 million-dollar venture. A grand hotel at Greenland Ranch to "tempt the jaded appetites of world globe trotters" had been contemplated by Smith for many years, but it was always his other businesses that kept his interest...and most of his money.

Borax Company executives weren't the only ones contemplating developing tourism in Death Valley. Herman William (Bob) Eichbaum, fresh from learning the hospitality business from William Wrigley the chewing gum king, began considering Death Valley as the perfect spot to develop a tourist trade. Eichbaum had lived in the Death Valley area during the Rhyolite gold boom and became quite familiar with the magical desert. He later worked with Wrigley on Catalina Island.

Bob Eichbaum with his wife Helene

Eichbaum made plans for a hotel high up at Hell's Gate on the route to Beatty, Nevada. Eichbaum knew the only way he could get tourists to Death Valley and his planned hotel would be to build them a decent auto road. Eichbaum was granted permission by the Inyo County supervisors to build a toll road from Darwin into the great valley.

Work to build the road was performed at break-neck speed with the first cut being completed in just two short months.

Eichbaum's road was an engineering marvel, allowing fairly safe passage for visitors to Death Valley in the comfort of their own auto

This 38-mile road was constructed over some of the most difficult terrain to be found. Nevertheless, the crew consisting of only one caterpillar tractor and six men with shovels completed their road in just a few short months. Eichbaum named it the Mt. Whitney Toll Road.

One of the major nearby attractions Eichbaum would showcase from his new hotel would be the magnificent Mesquite Sand Dunes. However, when the trucks carrying the lumber to build Eichbaum's hotel up at Hell's Gate got hopelessly mired in the sand from these dunes, Eichbaum decided to unload the trucks and build his hotel right there.

The Mesquite Sand Dunes have always been a popular
Death Valley destination

Road building costs cut deeply into Eichbaum's budget and his plans for a grand hotel had to be scaled back. Nevertheless, in November 1926, Eichbaum completed work on twenty neat, green and white tent cabins he christened Bungalette City. The awful and dangerous valley of death was finally open to tourism.

Bungalette City, later to be known as Stovepipe Wells Hotel, was the first hotel to do business in Death Valley

In 1913, a rancher drilling for water on his land 27 miles east of Mojave, California came upon a hard, crystalline material which proved to be Colemanite, a highly sought-after form of borax. Pacific Coast Borax Company quickly bought up all available land and mineral rights in this area and named it the Kramer District.

This new discovery of borax in the Kramer District was much closer to the company's refinery in Wilmington and a mine here would greatly reduce the transportation costs.

The Borax Company had heavily invested in railroads to haul the borax out of Death Valley, the standard-gauge Tonopah & Tidewater (T&T) and the narrow-gauge Death Valley Railroad. The T&T connected with the Union Pacific Railroad line near Ludlow, California, which hauled it the remaining distance to the Wilmington refinery.

With company profits setting records, Pacific Coast Borax made the decision to stay in Death Valley, at least for the time being. Much exploration and prep work would need to be done at the new discovery in Kramer and it would be years until the area would be ready for large-scale mining. But borax managers knew their time in Death Valley was coming to an end...or was it?

THE PLAYERS

Harry Gower grew up on his family's lemon farm in the Hollywood area of Los Angeles. As a young man, wanderlust struck Harry and he soon traveled about trying to find just the right spot to stop and stay awhile. In 1909, he ended up in Death Valley where he found a job with the firmly established Pacific Coast Borax Company which was expanding its operations at that time. Hard working and intelligent, Harry quickly worked his way up the Borax Company's corporate ladder and became the land superintendent of all the borax lands in the Death Valley area, a job he held until 1959. When the Borax Company eventually left Death Valley for Kramer, Harry stayed on to keep an eye on things, and skillfully guided the company and its interests into a new era of hotels and hospitality.

Borax Land Superintendent Harry Gower

Frank Jenifer got a job as a young man working as a freight agent on the Borax Company's Tonopah & Tidewater Railroad (T&T). When the California Railroad Commission refused to allow the Borax Company to sell more bonds to finance an expansion of their railroad to their new mine, the Borax Company created a new railroad, named it the Death Valley Railroad and made Jenifer its president. Jenifer oversaw construction of the 17-mile line which in itself was another engineering marvel. By 1926, Jenifer had become general manager of Pacific Coast Borax and later a vice president. He also became the president of the company's Death Valley Hotel subsidiary, which built and developed the Inn and Ranch at the Oasis at Death Valley. Jenifer was responsible for most of the decision making for building the hotels and his vision helped lay the groundwork for what is seen at the resort today.

Frank Jenifer was the Borax Company's Vice President as well as the president of its subsidiary, the Death Valley Hotel Company

Christian Brevoort Zabriskie was born at Fort Bridger, Wyoming Territory. He attended various schools while growing up and at a very early age went to work as a telegrapher for the Virginia & Truckee Railroad in Carson City, Nevada. He later worked in banking and even as a mortician in the mining camps.

Zabriskie was hired by F.M. Smith to supervise the workers at Smith's Candelaria, Nevada borax operation in 1885. This was the beginning of Zabriskie's life-long career with Pacific Coast Borax. Zabriskie worked hard and gained the favor of Smith as he helped lead the company to profitability. He eventually worked his way up to president and general manager and played an important part in taking the Borax Company into the hospitality industry.

C.B. Zabriskie was president of the Borax Company when the decision was made to get into the hospitality business

In 1925, Pacific Coast Borax made the decision to begin the move to the recently discovered deposits in the Kramer district (which soon came to be known as Boron) and close out their Death Valley operations. The company would leave behind an extensive railroad system in which they had invested millions of dollars in equipment and infrastructure.

The Borax Company would also leave behind the mining camp of Ryan, the community at Death Valley Junction with the roasting plant, and Greenland Ranch at Furnace Creek. All these areas had extensive developments from water systems to hundreds of thousands of square feet of office, residential and warehouse space.

The borax mining camp at Ryan was home to over 200 miners at its peak in the early 1920s

Executives at Pacific Coast Borax felt they couldn't completely walk away from all they had invested in Death Valley. Most of these men had lived and worked at these mines. They had become intimately familiar with the extraordinary Death Valley scenery. They had enjoyed and knew well the auspicious winter weather this desert region had to offer. The notion was bantered about that instead of hauling borax, perhaps their railroads could now carry tourists to Death Valley instead. And maybe…if they built a world class hotel right in this midst of all this scenic beauty, people would want to come visit this mysterious land.

In the photograph below, Borax officials are seen contemplating the company's future in Death Valley. DV Hotel Company president Frank Jenifer is second from left, Wash Cahill, general manager of the Tonopah & Tidewater Railroad is center and Christian Zabriskie is far right.

Borax executives contemplate the possibility of getting into the hospitality business in Death Valley

The company's British partners were consulted and there was consensus among everyone to build a Death Valley hotel. But where should they build it? Dare they take a chance and build their resort on the valley floor itself?

Nellie Coffman was the proprietress of the popular Desert Inn at Palm Springs, and a friend of Frank Jenifer. She was invited to Death Valley to offer her professional opinion on building a hotel there.

Coffman knew the desert and she knew tourism, and based upon her own experience, she said she was certain a hotel built at sea level right at the mouth of Furnace Creek Wash was just the right place. The Borax Company and its British investors agreed and work on the new hotel quickly began.

Nellie Coffman, proprietress of Palm Springs' Desert Inn Resort

The original Desert Inn was a small health resort built by Coffman along with her husband and two sons in 1908. Her skills in hospitality combined with her warm personality helped make the Desert Inn and Palm Springs a popular winter resort and a huge financial success. Tourists were coming from all over the world to enjoy the beauty and warm winter weather of the desert. She is often referred to as the "mother of Palm Springs."

Pacific Coast Borax executives believed a luxury hotel would have the most appeal. They wanted a resort that would become renowned throughout the world. Through business connections from their Los Angeles offices, Jenifer contacted one of the best-known west coast architects at the time, Albert C. Martin, to design their hotel.

Albert C. Martin was a leading west coast architect in the 1920s

By 1926, Martin already had designed a number of prestigious projects in California and his work was well underway on what would become one of his most famous works, the Los Angeles City Hall (below). Martin agreed to design a hotel for the Borax Company.

Plans were made to design the hotel and build it as quickly as possible. The hotel was to be of a California Mission style design made of stucco, a red tile roof and adobe bricks. It would be one of the largest adobe buildings built in the United States. By the end of summer 1926, native Paiutes and Shoshones worked feverishly manufacturing the bricks at the nearby Ranch and by November, all the needed adobe bricks had been cast.

The Borax Company found it impossible to find a contractor willing to come to such a remote and difficult location and workers generally did not stay long at the jobsite. It was very difficult to recruit the skilled craftsmen needed to build the new hotel.

Adobe bricks for construction of the Inn were cast at the Borax Company's Greenland Ranch

Water delivery system for the new resort

The Furnace Creek area is blessed to have two large springs with a combined flow of approximately 2,400 gallons of good water every minute. A 1,000-foot delivery system was built to bring the water to the hotel. Note in this picture some of the beautiful rockwork in this raceway.

On February 1, 1927, the Inn opened its door to the first guests. Work on the Inn had been completed in a whirlwind of just four months. It was simplistic yet very elegant in design with twelve neatly appointed sleeping rooms.

To provide services to their guest the hotel also featured a dining room, lobby and the necessary service rooms. Workers for the hotel stayed in tents below, in the wash. Construction workers were still putting on the final details as the first tourists arrived. Advertising literature invited tourists to "view the dire and dreadful Death Valley-with all dangers removed and all thrills retained."

The rockwork seen above was extensivly incorporated into all phases of the new hotel as it was expanded and enlarged over the next 10 years

The original Inn Dining Room was in part of the area that is now the reception lobby

The sleeping rooms were comfortable and very well appointed. Advertising brochures declared every room had a shower, bath and fireplace. When the hotel first opened in 1927, some of the sleeping rooms were located in the area that is now the Dining Room at the Inn.

"A fireplace in every room"

Pacific Coast Borax was intent on having everything perfect at their new hotel in Death Valley from the very start. They took no chances by hiring the best architect available and they followed suit when they hired Beulah Brown to be their first manager. Brown had already proved herself as the very capable manager of the prestigious Old Faithful Lodge in Yellowstone National Park during the summer months. Beulah also brought part of her Old Faithful summer staff with her to operate the Inn during its first two winter seasons. The Inn quickly became known far and wide for being at the forefront of offering exceptional customer service to their guests.

Brown was also very progressive thinking in the management of her staff. She felt the guests looked to the food servers, front desk people and bell persons as tour guides as well. Brown regularly sponsored outings and forays for the employees of the Inn, so they could speak knowingly to the guests about Death Valley's many scenic wonders.

The Inn's first manager Beulah Brown

Hoping to cash in on the popularity of Americans visiting National Parks and using passenger trains to do so, Pacific Coast Borax partnered with the Union Pacific Railroad to bring the first tourists to Death Valley. The plan was for the tourists to be brought to Crucero in the Mojave Desert, by the Union Pacific where they would transfer to the Borax Company's Tonopah and Tidewater line and then taken to Death Valley Junction. From the junction, tourists would travel the remaining 17 miles on a gasoline powered express-passenger car to the old mining camp of Ryan, which had been remodeled and refurbished into the Death Valley View Hotel. There, they would spend their first night in Death Valley and proceed the next morning to the Inn at the Oasis at Death Valley via tour bus provided by Union Pacific.

The borax mining camp of Ryan housed and fed over two-hundred miners during the peak of mining. It was decided the worker barracks could easily be converted to sleeping rooms for the arriving guests. The dining hall was made into the restaurant. The name Death Valley View Hotel was given because of the commanding view it had overlooking the valley.

The Union Pacific had already been promoting tourism in Bryce, Zion and the North Rim of the Grand Canyon for a number of years. They had made popular the "sing away" where hotel employees would line up and sing songs of gratitude and best wishes to the departing guests.

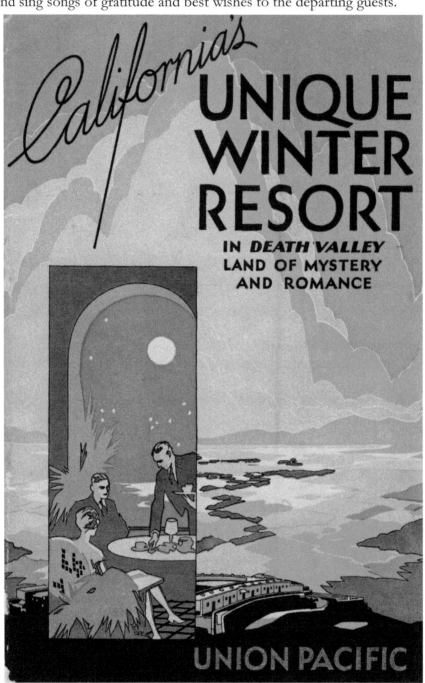

The Union Pacific Railroad brochure-1929

The final 17 miles from the Death View Hotel at Ryan to the Inn was over the Borax Company's old mining road in a Union Pacific touring car. The guides were usually young women and were well versed in the multitude of interesting facts and features of Death Valley.

Most of the roads in Death Valley at the time were old mining and service roads from the borax mining days. Having originally been built to be used by heavy equipment and wagons, they were not in the best of shape for travel by automobile.

Touring cars from Bryce and Zion were used in Death Valley

When the Inn opened in 1927, Death Valley enjoyed no protected status as a National Park or National Monument. It was merely a large expanse of California desert, best known for the mining of borax and for its morbid sounding name. There was no federal government to help build and maintain the roads. It was only the Borax Company (and Bob Eichbaum up the road at Bungalette City) that was promoting and advertising Death Valley as a place for tourists to come visit. The entire infrastructure for the hotel, water, roads, sewer and electricity had to be built, installed and maintained by the companies doing business there. It was an expensive proposition and a huge financial risk, and simply put, it was free enterprise and private investment working at its very best.

Just a few weeks before the Inn was scheduled to open, Borax Company executives realized they would need scenic outlooks, vistas and designated points of interest for the tourists to visit when they arrived. Land Superintendent Harry Gower quickly built and improved roads into a number of sites in Death Valley as the Inn was nearing completion. Just a few miles from the Inn was a spot that provided a panorama of colors and shapes overlooking the eroded badlands of the Funeral Mountains. It was the perfect place for a featured tourist stop. The top of a small hill was bladed flat and a steep road put in for cars to get to the top. The scenic vista was named Zabriskie Point in honor of the president of the Borax Company at the time, Christian Zabriskie.

Scenic view from Zabriskie Point

When borax and Union Pacific executives asked Shoshone businessman, politician and longtime Death Valley area resident Charles Brown if he knew of a good location for them to develop a scenic overlook, placid Brown shrugged, "I don't pay much attention to scenery, but I know one view that stopped and made me look." When he took them to it, they all agreed it was the most spectacular view of Death Valley any of them had seen. The view-spot loomed a mile above the lowest spot in the western hemisphere at Badwater. Telescope Peak rose majestically across the airy abyss and far off in the distance could be seen the Sierra Nevada mountains near Mt. Whitney, the highest spot in the continental United States. They named it Dantes View. Dutifully, Harry Gower built a winding, twisting road to provide access to the scenic spot. An enclosed observatory was also built at the site by Gower so guests could enjoy the view in comfort out of the sometimes chilly winter temperatures.

South of the Inn lies hills and canyons of varied colors and unusual formations. The Borax Company improved and rerouted an existing mining road here and named it Volcanic Drive. It was later renamed Artists Drive and is still a very popular destination for Death Valley visitors to enjoy.

The Borax Company promoted its scenic wonders in unique fashion...here are two young ladies hamming it up at Devils Golf Course

With such a flurry of road and infrastructure building, Pacific Coast Borax barely had enough left in their coffers to fund the operation of the Inn. If their venture into the hotel business was ever going to be profitable, they would need a partner to share the expenses. In 1927, there were already almost 20 national parks that were enticing tourists with their natural wonders. The borax men thought the beauty of Death Valley was certainly deserving of National Park status. Not to mention, a National Park would bring in the federal government to take care of the roads and infrastructure, promote and advertise to tourists and keep any additional hotel developers out. The Borax Company already had an ally in the newly created agency known as the National Park Service (NPS). Its director was Stephen Mather, who years earlier had worked for the Pacific Coast Borax Company and as their publicist, had introduced the very successful 20-Mule Team marketing campaign for their soap products. The assistant NPS Director at that time was Horace Albright, a local Inyo County boy raised in Bishop, California.

Horace Albright in wagon, Stephen Mather below with hat in hand, borax men Zabriskie to his right, Wash Cahill on far right

Ever the smart businessmen, Pacific Coast Borax Company executives began another very successful marketing campaign to promote not only their borax products, but also Death Valley and their hotels. In 1930, Death Valley Days was introduced on the radio, sponsored by the Borax Company. The show featured weekly dramas of events that allegedly happened in Death Valley.

Death Valley Days ran first on radio and then television for over 30 years

The weekly radio program became one of the most popular radio shows of its day and was on the air until 1945. In 1952, Death Valley Days was resurrected as a television show and ran until 1970. The show was hosted by a master of ceremonies known as the Old Ranger. The position was held by a number of different actors including Ronald Reagan in 1964-65.

The last employment Ronald Reagan had before he became governor of California was as the host of Death Valley Days

Stephen Mather passed away in 1930 and his assistant, Horace Albright took over as Director of the National Park Service. Horace had been raised in Bishop, California and was well familiar with Death Valley. Horace felt it very deserving of National Park status. He campaigned in congress to pass legislation to make Death Valley a park. However, with the Great Depression well underway, Congress was not in the mood to allocate scarce federal funds for preserving a new national park, especially one in the desert. Not to be deterred, Albright took up his campaign with his boss, President Herbert Hoover. Hoover also had his hands full with the nation's sinking economy but gave Albright his attention. Creation of a national park requires a vote of approval from Congress, something Albright wasn't going to be able to obtain. But the creation of a national monument can be done simply by Executive Order. Only the

President's signature would be required. Below, Albright (left) and Hoover can be seen enjoying some time in the great outdoors.

Herbert Hoover was voted out of office in November 1932. At that time, the newly elected president did not assume office until March. In one of his last actions as president, Hoover signed executive order #2028, setting aside almost two million acres of desert wilderness as Death Valley National Monument in February of 1933.

Horace Albright (L) and President Hoover (R)

Pacific Coast Borax created the Death Valley Hotel Company as a completely separate subsidiary to run their hotel operation. Borax vice president Frank Jenifer was made the new subsidiary's president. The budget for the first phase of construction for the Inn was about $40,000.

This financial statement by Pacific Coast Borax accountants (next page) was prepared about one month after the Inn opened in 1927 and shows actual costs exceeded budget by more than double. Jenifer blamed himself for these over-runs though there was very little he could have done to control them. Freight costs were extremely expensive and turnover among the workers was very high. The remote location and difficult working conditions made it difficult to recruit and keep help. A.C. Martin was the contractor as well as the architect for the first phase of the Inn. The Borax Company used its own workers for all the remaining construction and costs began to fall a little more in line.

FURNACE CREEK INN

CONSTRUCTION, ETC.

(To March 31, 1927)

	As of MARCH 31st 1927
INN CONSTRUCTION	
Main Building	53,570.30
Furniture, Fixtures and Equipment	12,764.28
Power House	633.00
Power House Equipment	4,874.97
Grading	3,324.89
Roads	318.34
Landscaping	803.95
Gasoline Tanks	271.14
Garage	364.59
Permanent Water Supply	2,067.51
Cooling Tower	40.51
Boarding House & Camp Operation	976.40
Temporary Water Supply	71.42
Supervision - Supt., Engineers, etc.	3,528.93
A. C. Martin, Architect fees	2,616.98
TOTAL INN CONSTRUCTION	86,229.21
OTHER CONSTRUCTION	
Dante's Point	
Roads, Rest Rooms, etc.	726.25
Salt Creek	
Rest Rooms	12.06
SALVAGE, ETC.	
Concrete Mixer and Tools, etc. on hand	1,187.56
Brick Tile, pipe, etc. on hand	416.30
Paints and Plaster " "	682.87
Cook Shack and Camp (Temporary)	1,766.44
TOTAL DISBURSEMENTS (To March 31,1927)	91,020.69

The Inn closed its first season in May of 1927. Over 1,200 guests had stayed at the new hotel in just over three months. By all accounts the Inn had a very successful first season and Pacific Coast Borax Company moved ahead with their planned expansion.

Not wanting to obscure the views from the existing building and to keep the lines of the building in symmetry, the next addition (known as the Terrace) would be built one level below the main building.

The Terrace Rooms at the Inn were built one level lower so as not to occlude the beautiful views from the main building

One year later the second phase of the terrace rooms was completed. The two wings were joined by a row of rooms across the west side and an additional two rooms were added to the east side of both wings. This brought the total guest rooms at the Inn to 32 by the beginning of the 1929 winter season.

It was an expensive proposition to build a hotel in such a remote and far off location. The estimate for the cost of construction for the second phase of the hotel by land superintendent Gower was $77,866. Today, this number would equal well over a million dollars. Gower voices confidence in keeping to budget in his closing remarks to Jenifer in this August 1927 letter (above).

COPY

August 10,1927

VIA AIR MAIL

Mr.F.M.Jenifer,
Pacific Coast Borax Co.,
100 William St.,
New York,N.Y.

Dear Frank:

I called at Mr.Martins office yesterday and with Mr.Gilbert worked out a rough estimate of what the new addition as planned at Furnace Creek will cost.

Prices of materials run practically the same now as last winter,so we made the estimate using last year's costs as a basis. The present building covers 10338 sq.ft. in actual construction not including grading,rubble work,etc. giving us a cost of $5.34 per sq.ft.

The addition has a slightly larger area - 10,780 sq.ft., and at $5.34 per sq.ft. will cost $57,565.00. To this,of course, we must add the putting up and maintaining a camp for several months, also the grading and landscaping of the grounds and possibly the added cost of the trench which we will put under the building for the sewer and water pipes. This would give us an estimate as follows:

Concrete lined trench for plumbing:	$1500.00
Actual construction @ $5.34 per sq.ft:	57,565.20
Grading:	4000.00
Landscaping {Walks {Walks {Terraces	4000.00
Camp:	1000.00
TOTAL	$68,065.20

We discussed this figure with Mr.Martin and he said that it was quite proper to base the estimate on last years work as that is all we have to go on. He,however,added 10% to the above for miscellaneous and unforeseen expenses and also his fee of 4% on the total,making:

Estimated total:	$68,065.20
Miscellaneous:	6,806.50
4% to architect:	2,994.30
Total	$77,866.00

Personally,I feel that we can give you a first-class job and not touch the amount allowed for miscellaneous expenses.

Yours very truly,

H.P.GOWER

Despite being one of the driest places in the world, the Furnace Creek area of Death Valley actually has an abundance of good fresh water. Travertine Springs and Texas Springs are located about a mile from the Inn. The combined volume of the two springs is approximately 2,400 gallons of water every minute. The springs are also "warm water" springs, with water coming out of the ground at about 87°F.

The first pool in the area was built early during construction of the Inn. It was located up the wash next to Travertine Springs and was for use by both employees and guests. The only problem, it was a mile drive by car and then a walk to get to it. The Borax Company knew it would eventually need a pool at the Inn itself for the convenience of its guests.

The first pool in the Furnace Creek area was located about a mile from the Inn, next to the main springs themselves

Once the terrace rooms were completed, Pacific Coast Borax began to make plans for a world class pool at the Inn. Taking advantage of the huge abundance of natural warm water, the design was for the pool to be "flow-through," meaning water would be allowed to flow out of it as fast as it could flow in.

A flow-through pool meant sanitation levels could be maintained without the need to add chemicals. The water exiting the pool would travel one mile through an open ditch to irrigate the all grass golf course as well as other landscaping at the Ranch. The entire volume of water at the pool would changeover several times each day. The beautiful pool was meant to be one of the prime highlights of a guest's stay.

The pool itself was lined with sky blue tile. Two small children pools were built next to the main pool though they were removed a few years later and replaced with grass. The pool also featured a diving board and two diving platforms. The beautiful rockwork around the pool as well as most of the Inn is the work of stone mason Dobie Gunnarson and his partner Serafin Esteves. The beautiful archways that frame the desert views to the west add to the wonderful contrast of the scene. Two huge fireplaces would keep guests warm while swimming in the evening.

181- Swimming Pool. Furnace Creek Inn, Death Valley, Cal.

Beauituful stone masonary work is one of the many hallmarks of the Inn

The pool was enormously popular with the hotel guests. With Death Valley's pleasant winter temperatures, the pool was always busy. Resort staff and Park Service employees were allowed to use the pool as well. In later years, massage rooms, gym, a sauna, a bar and snack shop were added to the pool's amenities.

Visitation at the Furnace Creek Inn continued to climb. The hotel was more often than not sold out during its season which was generally mid-October to mid-May. The Borax Company thought they could sell even more rooms to guests if they had them available. The two-story north wing with 21 rooms was added in 1930.

The Inn was evolving into a destination of its own. The beautiful design of the hotel combined with its jaw dropping views created an atmosphere where many guests were content to enjoy Death Valley solely from the premises of the Inn. The building of the north wing placed a substantial amount of desert directly in front of the hotel. Harry Gower thought with its abundance of water, the resort should landscape the desert hillsides in front of the hotel into a green and lush garden and allow water to flow through it as a creek with ponds and small waterfalls. Fan palms and Deglect Noor date palms were planted on the hillsides encompassing the sloping gulch. Flowers, shrubs and other varieties of vegetation were added to enhance the pastoral scene.

Beautiful landscaping helped transform the Inn into a true Oasis

As the Inn added more sleeping rooms, the original dining room and lobby area were not large enough to adequately serve all the guests at the hotel. It was decided to take out ten of the sleeping rooms from the original south wing of the hotel and convert this space into an expanded and larger dining room. And by removing the original dining room from its current location, a large area would be freed up to expand the hotel lobby for the comfort of Inn guests. The new dining room could seat approximately 120, and six large windows provided guests with stupefying views of Death Valley. The chef usually offered a rotating menu for dinner featuring a five-course meal that was included in the guest's American plan hotel rate. Inn chefs and cooks often worked at other resorts in the summer when the Inn was closed.

The beautiful Inn Dining Room offered fine dining cuisine that matched the incredible desert views

Continuing to take advantage of the great winter weather, the Inn would often feature outside dining events. In the picture on the next page, Chef Bob McGovern is carving up turkey at a Thanksgiving dinner being served at the Inn gardens in the 1930s. A lot of work for the staff, but a real crowd pleaser for guests of the Inn.

Inn Chef Bob McGovern serving up Thanksgiving dinner at the Inn gardens

The lobby area of the hotel also afforded incredible views overlooking the desert with several large windows to take it all in. Though not large, the lobby featured a simple elegance that blended perfectly the use of rock, tile, wood and light.

Johnny Mills was an old-time prospector who first came to Death Valley in 1896. The Borax Company put him on the payroll at the Inn. His job was to tarry in the lobby, tell stories and answer questions about Death Valley. Johnny had his own version of many Death Valley tales, which provided great entertainment for the guests of the Inn.

Old time prospector Johnny Mills was hired by the Borax Company to entertain Inn guests with stories of Death Valley

The Inn at the Oasis at Death Valley seemed to put together just the right components to create a nostalgic and romantic attraction that developed into a passionate zeal for its guests. The Inn began enjoying repeat business from its very first year. Many guests started to think of the Inn as their own, requesting and reserving certain rooms a year in advance.

With up to 150 people staying at the hotel on busy nights, the Borax Company felt they should provide nightly entertainment for their guests. A large recreation room was constructed below the terrace rooms and above the pool. This location did not block the existing vista, and offered its own views of not only the majestic desert and mountains, but also the dazzling new Inn pool. The beautiful terrazzo floor and rock work can be seen in the photo below.

The beautiful "Gold Rush" room as it is now named, was originally a recreation room, where movies, ranger programs and other forms of entertainment were offered to guests of the Resort

Not all the guest activities offered by the Resort were at the Inn. During its heyday, the old mining camp at Ryan had operated a baby gauge rail line to haul borax out of the mines. Once tourism began and the mining ceased, the Borax Company converted some of the old ore cars to passenger cars and visitors to Death Valley were treated to a thrilling eight-mile trip through the old borax mine works. The "Baby Gauge" (next page) offered rides off and on to Death Valley visitors up until the early 1950s. A preserved and working set of this historic rail line is kept at Ryan Camp today.

The Baby Gauge thrilled Death Valley visitors up until the early 1950s

The Baby Gauge was very popular, but the other Death Valley railroads were not. Tourists never did catch on to the idea of taking the train to Death Valley. No matter what the condition of the roads, they preferred to drive their own cars. By 1930, the Borax Company gave up on the idea of offering rail service to Death Valley.

Visitors drove their own cars to Death Valley even before the construction of improved roads

Prohibition came to an end in 1933 and the Inn wasted no time in providing a location for its guests to enjoy a cocktail. The picture above shows the first and quite cramped cocktail lounge at the Inn. In a bold move, the hillside underneath the existing dining room was excavated to build not only a larger lounge, but a second restaurant as well. In order to hold up the dining room during excavation, the Borax Company dismantled a railroad trestle on the now defunct rail line, used the huge timbers to hold up the building and ultimately incorporated them into the structure itself (seen in picture below).

Golf was another amenity the Oasis at Death Valley wanted to provide for its guests. One mile to the west of the Inn, on the very floor of Death Valley itself was Greenland Ranch. It was 480 acres of flat land with plenty of water that had already been planted with alfalfa. It was thought the perfect location to build a golf course. During the early fall of 1929, the Borax Company built an all grass, 9-hole course for the enjoyment of its guests. At 214 feet below sea level, it was and still is the lowest grass golf course in the world and the first course in the California desert region. It had several water hazards and offered stunning views of the surrounding desert and mountains. Golfers pose for a picture in front of the clubhouse/pro-shop in the picture at top of page.

The golf course was very popular, even with the park rangers (seated)

Realizing the time and effort it took to get to Furnace Creek in 1929, Pacific Coast Borax Company built an airport down on the desert floor just east of Greenland Ranch. Guests could now get to Death Valley quickly if they had access to a plane. Here is Resort manager Charlie Scholl giving title to the airport to the National Park Service in the 1950s.

The original airport was located where Sunset Campground is today. In the 1930s, several charter airlines offered service to Death Valley, and for a short time, Las Vegas based Bonanza Airlines even offered scheduled commercial service to the desert Oasis (below).

Despite growing ever more popular with the traveling public, advertisers were still using Death Valley as a whipping boy to validate just how durable their products were. Here is a General Electric advertisement from the 1930s touting how their refrigerators and water coolers work well even in the extremes of Death Valley.

But nothing could stop the flood of people attracted to seeing Death Valley. By the 1928-29 winter season, more than 10,000 people visited the once feared and ominous valley. In 1935 there were 45,000 visitors and by 1941 110,000 people a year were making their way to Death Valley National Monument.

Once Death Valley National Monument was created, the Park Service, with the assistance of the Civilian Conservation Corp, improved roads, placed more infrastructure and built several campgrounds.

Clark Gable and Carole Lombard

From the beginning, the resort attracted the rich and famous. The Inn's reputation for luxury was such that…after secretly marrying in Arizona in 1939, Clark Gable and Carole Lombard, both huge stars at the time, honeymooned at the Inn. *Gone with The Wind* debuted the following year.

The Inn and later, the Ranch at the Oasis at Death Valley provided accommodations for the actors and film crews during the filming of many of the movies and TV shows filmed in Death Valley. And not surprisingly, many of the stars returned to enjoy the resort after filming.

At first there was William Powell, Claudette Colbert, Bette Davis and John Barrymore. Later, Marlon Brando, Martin Sheen, Matt Damon, Kurt Russell, Goldie Hawn, Diane Keaton as well as many others would stay and relax at the magnificent oasis. Anthony Quinn enjoyed the Resort so much, he held large family reunions at the Inn for a number of years.

As more and more of Hollywood's famous stars frequented the Inn, paparazzi would often hang around the hotel hoping to get a photo of one of the celebrities during their stay.

The decision made by Pacific Coast Borax Company to get into the hospitality business seemed to have been a good one. It is interesting to note that the rapid growth of visitation to the new resort and Death Valley occurred even while the country was experiencing the worst of the Great Depression.

The Inn had an appeal to a certain class of visitor. The rate for double occupancy at the Inn in 1930 was $15, a very high price for its day. Prices at the Inn were not that affordable to a large segment of the population and the Borax Company knew it. Was there a market for accommodations in Death Valley that would appeal to the broader spectrum of the traveling public?

The Inn pool-a touch of class and elegance

 *FOUR*

Down on the Ranch

In 1930, the decision had been made to no longer promote the usage of the Borax Company's railroads as a method for tourists to travel to Death Valley. This left the old miner barracks at Ryan that had been converted into the Death Valley View Hotel, without a direct means for guests to travel there. Though business at the hotel was never significant, it did act as an overflow for the Inn during busy holiday and weekend periods. At this same time, Frank Jenifer, Harry Gower and others felt a more affordable place to stay in the Valley to, "balance out the high class patronage the Inn was attracting" should be built.

Greenland Ranch, with its level land and abundance of water was chosen as just the right spot. The Borax Company moved 18 tent cabins that had been used as a construction camp while building the Inn, down to a cleared area at Greenland Ranch. These tents became the Ranch's first lodging for guests. The name was changed to Furnace Creek Camp and the Borax Company opened their second hotel in Death Valley.

Furnace Creek Camp was a working ranch before being developed for tourism

Twenty one-room corrugated sided cabins (below) from the Borax Company's Gertsley mine near Shoshone were soon brought to Furnace Creek Camp for additional guest accommodations. These cabins, later referred to as the "sizzlers," were not insulated and a bit uncomfortable when the Death Valley weather turned warm. They were used for guest accommodations and employee housing up until the 1970s.

Business at the Camp was brisk from the very start and it was enlarged several times over the next ten years. A kitchen, dining room, general store, recreation hall and horse stables were all added to accommodate the hundreds of guests that would stay nightly at the new property. Furnace Creek Camp was soon renamed Furnace Creek Ranch.

Not far from Death Valley lies Boulder City, Nevada. The great Boulder Dam was completed just a few years after the Furnace Creek Ranch opened. When the dam was finished, the Six Companies Inc, as the contractors for the dam were known, had a huge number of housing units they had built for their construction workers, that they were now selling off as surplus. Pacific Coast Borax got wind of the deal and sent Harry Gower to Boulder City to buy a few. The Borax Company picked up 20 small cabins (below) for one dollar each and brought them back to the Ranch with their mining trucks. They were first rented to visitors as efficiency cabins where guests would often stay for months at a time. The cabins are still in use today as employee housing.

When the Ranch first opened in 1930, Edna Boswell and her sister-in-law Mary, the wives of the Ranch foreman and mechanic, managed the new Death Valley resort. After two years, Clyde and Bess Erskine (pictured below), who worked under the tutelage of Beulah Brown at the Inn and Old Faithful Lodge took over and successfully oversaw the Ranch operations for the next ten years.

Cabins placed along the state highway were first used for staff. Below, Ranch employee Christine Watts is shown with her beau Everett outside their cabin. These cabins are still in great shape. The corrugated metal siding has been replaced, the rooms refurbished and are now used to accommodate guests at the Ranch.

Ranch employees Everett & Christine Watts-1940

Furnace Creek Ranch had already operated as Greenland Ranch for almost 50 years before it became a tourist resort. One of its primary functions was to grow alfalfa to raise the cattle to feed the miners at the borax camps. In the early 1920s, borax executives thought the addition of date palms at the Ranch might bring in additional revenue. It took a bit to master the correct methods for pollination, but soon the date orchard flourished and the Ranch had over 1,500 trees under cultivation producing 200 tons of fruit annually. Several varieties were grown but it was determined the Deglect Noor was the best suited for Death Valley's climate. The U.S. Department of Agriculture even operated an experimental station here for a time in the 1920s.

The date orchard did so well at the Ranch, the Borax Company decided to plant a second orchard near the Inn. Here in this rare photo (below) you can see several dozen small date palms. The Inn date orchard was short lived and abandoned by the early 1940s.

Electricity for the Inn was first provided by a Pelton water wheel-generator that ran off the power developed from the flow of nearby Travertine Springs. As the Resort grew, more electricity was needed and a huge diesel generator was put in place at the Ranch (below). The building to the left is still being used now as part of the Resort's maintenance department.

Prior to the development of the Oasis at Death Valley hotels, the foreman at Greenland Ranch was one of the few year-round positions in Death Valley. It is claimed the foreman and the other summer workers would wrap themselves in wool blankets and lie in the irrigation ditch to cool themselves sufficiently to sleep. The foreman position was an important job and the Borax Company wanted to make life as easy as it could be in this harsh summer environment. This huge home at the Ranch (below) was for the foreman, and later the Ranch resort manager.

Death Valley was a great distance from anywhere. Every vehicle that arrived in Death Valley needed to refuel in order to get back to the next town. Here is a picture showing the original gasoline station at the Ranch, beautifully constructed out of native stone. A second gas station was built a mile away, across from the Inn.

In the 1930s, automobiles were not as reliable as they are today and guests often found the need for a mechanic once they arrived in Death Valley. The Resort built a huge garage across from the Inn staffed with as many as four mechanics and a couple of tow trucks at its peak. As cars became more reliable, the need for a full-service garage waned and the Resort converted the garage to a commercial laundry to take care of its need for clean sheets, towels and tablecloths. There was also a hairdresser and the Resort's nurse that occupied the front offices of this structure. A doctor would usually fly in once a week from Lone Pine to take care of the more serious illnesses.

The site of the former garage has recently been transformed into the Resort's beautiful new outdoor event venue-The Mission Gardens

What would a ranch be without horses? A stable was put in place at the Ranch very soon after it opened. Bruce Morgan, a rancher and stable operator from Lone Pine was contracted by the Borax Company to provide horses for guest use. Guided horse and carriage rides were offered, and guests could rent horses by the hour and head out on their own as well. Below is Morgan (front right) and a few guests posing with the Inn in the background. Bottom photo is Ranch employee Christine Watts (center) with a few friends enjoying a ride in the hills above the Inn on a couple of rented steeds.

The Timbisha-Shoshone Tribe had a settlement just south of Furnace Creek Ranch. The Tribe had lived in the Death Valley region for over a thousand years. When the National Monument was created in 1933, the tribe's homeland was subsumed by the monument boundary and no provision was made for an official reservation. Tribal members worked for the Resort and for the Park Service. Their children attended the school at the Ranch. Some members sold handmade items at small shops at their settlement.

The local Native Americans have been a very large part of the Death Valley community. Their numbers have fluctuated between seventy-five to one hundred and fifty members. Finally, after years of talks, legislation was enacted by the U.S. Congress in 2000 providing for the return of 7,500 acres of their ancestral home in and around Death Valley. Their settlement just south of the Ranch is now recognized as an official reservation.

As visitation at the Ranch grew, the Resort built a first-class warm water pool at this location as well. The same design for the Inn was used at the Ranch making it a flow-through pool, with the water running out as fast as it flowed in. The changeover in the volume of water was sufficient to meet county and state sanitation requirements without the use of chemicals.

A restaurant and store at the Ranch were built in the mid-1930s and were refurbished, remodeled and enlarged several times over the years as business steadily increased. This view of the commercial buildings is looking south from the parking lot behind the old Ranch service station.

The front desk registration-reception area for the Ranch was located in the east portion of the main commercial building. Notice the beautiful furnishings in this picture. The Borax Company maintained a sense of refinement at both of their Death Valley properties.

The original Ranch dining room was at the very west end of the main building. It was enlarged several times to meet the needs of the growing numbers of visitors to the new property.

Old Dinah was a mining steam tractor that had a short-lived life in Death Valley. Its rear wheel would dig in at soft sandy areas and was forever getting stuck. It finally broke down near Stovepipe Wells (Bungalette City) where the Borax Company abandoned it. Once Bob Eichbaum opened his hotel for tourists, Old Dinah become one of the attractions Eichbaum would take his guests to see. After the Borax Company opened their new Resort, they wanted to gussy up their property with old mining relics. Old Dinah fit the part. In a midnight raid, Harry Gower and a few Furnace Creek employees made claim to their abandoned property and dragged Old Dinah across the desert back to the Ranch for the enjoyment of their guests.

Scotty's Castle, the elaborate Death Valley home associated with con man extraordinaire Walter Scott, aka Death Valley Scotty, and built by millionaire Albert Johnson, was about 55 miles north of Furnace Creek. The Castle was built about the same time as the Inn. So many visitors were interested in what Johnson had built in such a remote location that he began to offer tours. Death Valley Scotty would often greet visitors in person, show them around the "Castle" and entertain them with his many tall tales. Below-right is a picture of Scotty with Awilda Scholl.

The Johnsons created their own religious, non-profit organization, the Gospel Foundation. Upon their death, the Johnsons left the Castle to the Foundation which rented out rooms to help defray the huge maintenance costs. The Foundation struggled to operate the Castle until 1970, when it sold the Castle, the land and all its furnishing to the National Park Service who has operated it ever since. Death Valley Scotty passed away in 1954.

World War II put a temporary halt to the explosion of tourism that Death Valley had experienced from the late 1920s through the 1930s. Gas rationing made it difficult to travel and combined with a shortage of labor, caused all Death Valley hotels to close at the end of the season in May of 1942. Caretakers kept a watch on the hotels. Some of the Park Service buildings were used to intern a few Japanese Americans from Manzanar Internment Camp near Independence. But other than that, Death Valley was closed.

The growth of tourism had happened so fast that managers at both the Inn and the Ranch spent a good deal of their time just trying to keep their heads above the flood of visitors that had descended upon Death Valley National Monument. Though the entire country was well involved in the effort to win the war, borax executives found time to catch their collective breath and ascertain what direction they would take once the war had ended. It was clear to all that tourism and Death Valley would forever be intertwined.

FIVE

Setting the Standard

Even without guests at their hotel, the war years were an active time at the Oasis at Death Valley. At the outbreak, Borax Consolidated of the United Kingdom still owned a majority interest in the Borax Company. In virtually all of the National Parks and Monuments the federal government owned the hotels and the land they were located on. The government would lease the buildings to private businesses which in turn would operate the business as a concessionaire.

The hotels at the Oasis at Death Valley were an exception. They were built by the Borax Company on their private land and were still owned by the Borax Company on their private land. For a time, the federal government considered taking title to both hotels from the British as part of the Lend Lease Act that provided assistance to our ally during World War II. The transfer never happened, and the Resort readied itself for a new wave of tourists once the war was over. Above is a letter from a carpet maintenance company hoping to obtain work at the Borax Company's hotels as the war was coming to an end.

After the war ended, Death Valley Hotel Company executives and managers were excited to be back in business. This picture (below) was taken shortly after their hotels in Death Valley had re-opened. Their enthusiasm is quite evident. L-R Frank Jenifer, Fred Lesser, Mrs. Lesser, Mrs. Grim, Pace Grim, Mrs. Jenifer, Pauline Gower and Charlie Scholl.

The Inn and Ranch at the Oasis at Death Valley reopened their doors to guests on November 1, 1945. Enough maintenance had been performed during the shutdown that both hotels were in pretty good shape. With travel severely limited for the previous three and a half years, Americans were ready to hit the road and visits to the National Parks and Monuments were high on their list.

Many soldiers returning home after serving in Europe and the Pacific during the war had developed a new level of sophistication. The hospitality industry needed to meet the higher expectations travelers were bringing with them on their visits. Here's a late 1940s brochure showing fun and luxury (left) to be had at the Resort and an all-inclusive guided tour (right).

Americans began to develop a serious interest in golf and new courses were being built throughout the country. The golf course at the Ranch enjoyed increased usage due to the incredible scenery it could offer as well as the novelty of playing below sea level. A golf pro was added and tee times became scarce on busy weekends.

Longtime Death Valley Hotel Company employee Charlie Scholl (left) became the manager of the Inn after World War II. Scholl got his start as a bellman working at the Borax Company's Amargosa Hotel and had worked his way up to manager. He had also assisted at both Oasis at Death Valley properties during the 1930s. As the Resort entered a new era after the war, Scholl helped bring the properties into the modern age and served dutifully as General Manager up until the late 1950s. He then worked at the corporate offices in Los Angeles for a few years until his retirement.

Though no longer mining in the area, the Borax Company kept close ties with its Death Valley properties. Below is a banquet of Borax Company executives and Death Valley Hotel Company managers. In the center of this photo facing camera are Inn Manager Charlie Scholl, his wife Awilda to his right and Harry Gower next to her.

California was going to observe 100 years of statehood in 1949. The State formed a Centennial Commission to help various regions put on a birthday bash. In November of 1948, representatives from Inyo, Kern, San Bernardino and Los Angeles counties met in Ridgecrest, California to plan their region's celebration. T.R. Goodwin, superintendent of Death Valley National Monument urged the group to consider Death Valley for the location and from this meeting came the decision, to hold their centennial event in the deepest depths of Death Valley. To organize and manage the affair, the Death Valley '49er organization was created. Funds for the event had to be obtained, a program needed to be put together and the entire event was going to require an enormous amount of planning and organization.

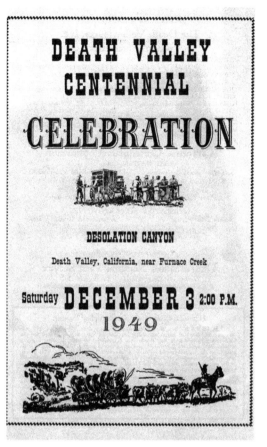

When the event was held in December of 1949, estimates range from 65,000 to 100,000 revelers came to celebrate the states 100th birthday. The roads in Death Valley became completely gridlocked.

Jimmy Stewart, who was staying at the Inn and was the Master of Ceremonies for the pageant, had to be taken across the desert in an army jeep that manager Scholl was able to round up, to get to the pageant five miles away. Governor Earl Warren was nearly lost in the massive crowds. The service stations ran out of fuel causing people to be stranded in Death Valley for days after the pageant ended. Then the store ran out of groceries as people waited for the gasoline to arrive. With thousands of people with no fuel and no groceries, Scholl had the chefs at the Ranch and the Inn put together soup and sandwich lines to feed the stranded attendees. In the end, no one went hungry, and by all accounts, everyone had a great time.

In 1954, Resort manager Charlie Scholl and Park Superintendent Goodwin decided Death Valley should have a museum. Scholl brought an old borax mining office building built in 1883 to the Ranch and placed artifacts, photos and Harry Gower's mineral collection inside. Old mining equipment and the now defunct narrow gauge railroad locomotive were placed in an outside yard at Death Valley's first museum, which was christened the Borax Museum.

After the 1949 Centennial Celebration, the Death Valley '49ers became a permanent organization whose stated purpose was to support Death Valley and all it had to offer. Though the new Borax Museum at the Ranch was popular and helped fill a void, it was small with very limited space. Officers from the '49ers met with park service and Borax Company officials about building a new and much bigger museum. Everyone agreed. In a joint effort, the '49ers, NPS and Borax Company came up with the funds for the Furnace Creek Visitor Center.

In 1952, wanting to replace some of the older lodging units at the Ranch, the Borax Company again contacted architect A.C. Martin and this time asked him to prepare a design for new rooms at their casual property. His design (below) was very modernistic incorporating a space age look that was a few years ahead of its time.

PROPOSED   EXPANSION   OF   GUEST   FACILITIES   AT

Furnace   Creek   Ranch

FOR   PACIFIC   COAST   BORAX   COMPANY

Martin's design was a little too futuristic for borax executives, especially for a hotel with the name "ranch" in it. Another architect was contracted, and a simpler motel room style was settled upon (below). Known as the Parksides because of their location on the Ranch's large grassy area, these were the first new lodging units built at the Ranch and are still very popular with guests today.

Seeing a potential at the Ranch to go beyond being merely a motel for guests visiting Death Valley, executives intended to transform the Ranch into a destination resort. Many amenities were added including the addition of tennis courts and an expansion of the golf course to 18-holes. The larger golf course was completed in 1968.

In the mid-1970s, the Resort engaged in the largest expansion to that date at its Death Valley properties. Four two-story modern motel buildings (below) with 40 rooms each were built on or near the now 18-hole golf course. Many of the rooms offered jaw-dropping views of the Panamint Mountains.

Despite averaging the lowest annual rainfall in North America, water plays a very important part in the Death Valley milieu. Infrequent summer monsoon storms bring isolated cells of intense amounts of precipitation. As little as half an inch of rain falling in a short period can send walls of waters several feet deep roaring down normally dry washes.

As California state highway 190 comes in from the east, it follows the natural drainage of Furnace Creek Wash. When flash floods happen in this area, they almost always affect the highway in one way or another. Fortunately, the California Department of Transportation is very efficient in quick road repair. This picture below shows damage done to Highway 190 from an August 2004 cloudburst.

Up until the early 1960s, all the electricity used in Death Valley was provided by a diesel generator or a Pelton water wheel. Around 1962, the electric company erected transmission lines right into the heart of Death Valley, and alas…the resorts had all the electricity they needed to operate at full capacity even during the intense heat of the summer months.

Gradually at first, and then steadily in greater and greater numbers, visitors started to come to the Oasis at Death Valley in the summer months to experience the extremes Death Valley had to offer. Most of the guests in June-September are from Europe and at the Oasis at Death Valley during that time of year, more than a dozen different languages may be heard. More people now visit Death Valley in August than any other month of the year.

International visitors were not the only people coming to Death Valley during the summer. Auto manufacturers from the United States and around the world began bringing next year's prototypes to Death Valley to test their worthiness in extreme summer conditions. The cars are often camouflaged to hide the next year's body styles.

In 1994 the U.S. Congress passed legislation that gave Death Valley, National Park status and enlarged its size to 3.3 million acres, making it the largest National Park in the contiguous United States. Due to its crystal-clear air and distance from major metropolitan areas, Death Valley National Park harbors some of the darkest night skies in the United States. That dark sky is key to its certification as the third International Dark Sky Park in the U.S. National Park System.

Included in the enlargement of Death Valley are two scenic treasures of particular note, the Eureka Sand Dunes and Saline Valley. The Eureka Dunes are among the tallest dunes in North America at almost 700 feet high. Five species of endemic beetles and three special plants have their entire range limited to this island of sand in Death Valley.

The Eureka Dunes are among the tallest in North America

Saline Valley is an area of natural hot springs, extreme beauty and is located in one of the most remote areas in the contiguous United States.

Death Valley's Saline Valley is far off the beaten track, and provides visitors with a true wilderness experience

 *Six*

The Beauty of Their Dreams

After World War II, the demand for borax continued to rise. The use of the white gold of the desert in producing a number of industrial compounds used in manufacturing had grown significantly. Its use as an additive in laundry soap was now miniscule compared to its varied other uses.

By 1956, the world's consumption of borax had grown to levels that took almost the entire focus of the Borax Company to keep up with the production needed to meet the demand.

Fred Harvey (next page) got his start by operating lunch counters for the Santa Fe Railroad in the late 1800s and his business grew to become a leader in the hospitality industry, owning or managing a number of resorts and hotels, including legendary El Tovar at the Grand Canyon. In 1956, the Borax Company asked the Fred Harvey Company to take over management of their Death Valley properties, so it could focus entirely on its mining.

Fred Harvey Company managed the Borax Company's hotels until 1968. At that time, after 40 years in the hospitality business, the Borax Company, now known as U.S. Borax, made the decision to sell the Inn and Ranch properties outright to the Fred Harvey Company.

Also in 1968, Amfac (American Factors), a land development company and sugar cane producer from Hawaii, bought the Fred Harvey Company including the Oasis at Death Valley.

Fred Harvey

Fred Harvey Company operated hotels throughout the Southwest

In 1988, JMB Realty Corporation from Chicago purchased Amfac and in 2002, the name was changed to Xanterra Parks & Resorts. The name Xanterra is derived from "Xanadu," a beautiful, idyllic paradise described in the poem *Kubla Khan* by Samuel Taylor Coleridge, and "terra," the Latin word for earth. Thus, Xanterra means "Beautiful Places on Earth."

In the early 1990s, Xanterra took a leadership position in addressing climate change as it became increasingly apparent that the warming of the world's oceans and other signs of climate change were having a dangerous and disturbing impact on National Parks.

Since 2000, the company has reduced total fossil fuel consumption company-wide by 29 percent and decreased greenhouse gas emissions by 27.5 percent. In 2004 Xanterra became one of the initial signatory members of the World Wildlife Fund Climate Savers program and the only national park concessioner to commit to the program's goals.

As an environmentally conscious steward of the nation's National Parks, Xanterra has developed several projects designed to reduce its carbon footprint. In 2008, Xanterra installed a one mega-watt photovoltaic system at the Ranch at the Oasis at Death Valley (below). The system produces more than one third of the electricity used by the resort and is one of the largest privately owned solar photovoltaic energy systems in the United States. The impressive facility eliminates the emission equivalent of 5,100 automobiles. In 2018, Xanterra upgraded this installation to 1.8 mega-watts, and this additional electricity will come on line in 2019.

The solar production facility at the Ranch is one of the largest privately owned solar generating operations in the United States

Encouraged by its success in Death Valley, Xanterra recently installed a solar array at its 12,000' above sea level Trail Ridge Store in Rocky Mountain National Park (next page). This system provides 100% of the facility's electricity needs. Xanterra has designed and developed energy conservation projects at a number of the facilities it owns and operates and has received numerous national, state and local awards for its energy conservation programs.

In 2008, the Anschutz Corporation purchased Xanterra. Owner Philip Anschutz knew early in life that he was put on earth to be a collector of businesses. The epiphany for Anschutz came at the historic Broadmoor Hotel, a Mediterranean-style resort built in 1918 at the base of Cheyanne Mountain in Colorado Springs, Colorado. "I started coming here when I was 5," he recalls. "And when I was 10, I was sitting in the corner of the bar when I told my mother and father, I was going to buy the Broadmoor some day."

And in 2011, Phillip Anschutz did just that. Combined with the legendary properties owned or managed by Xanterra, the Anschutz Corporation is responsible for some of the most iconic and historic properties in the United States, including the hotels and lodges at Yellowstone, Glacier, Grand Canyon, the Broadmoor in Colorado and of course, Death Valley.

Xanterra is now known as Xanterra Travel Collection and has diversified into additional hospitality and tourism related ventures including Windstar Cruises, American Railway Explorer, Country Walkers and many more. Xanterra Travel Collection remains the largest concession operator in the National Park system including operations at Glacier National Park, Zion, Yellowstone, Grand Canyon, Mt Rushmore, Rocky Mountain and Death Valley.

Shortly after the Anschutz Corporation bought Xanterra in 2008, the new owner took inventory of the numerous properties in the company's portfolio. Many of the hotels and resorts had been built decades earlier and were in need of rehabilitation and renovation. The Oasis at Death Valley was one of the properties chosen for improvements.

OZ Architecture, an award-winning, national architecture and design firm, was brought in to lead a major renovation of this unique resort destination. Beginning in 2017, the historic property underwent a significant transformation that brought a variety of new luxury amenities and facilities, while maintaining the historic ambiance, stylistic qualities and mission architecture that have attracted visitors for over 90 years.

Ever since the Inn opened in 1927, there was a parking lot directly in front of the hotel which significantly impacted its million-dollar view of Death Valley. The recent renovation has seen the parking removed and replaced with a beautifully landscaped small park (below). Guests can now sit on the deck in front of the Inn, with nothing in their viewshed but the beauty of Mother Nature.

The setting at the Inn has been further enhanced with vine draped pergolas, misters, archways, awnings and welcoming terraces gracing the historic property. A new cabana laden pool area showcases a pool café, deluxe massage rooms, a renovated fitness center and sauna.

Additional renovations have been made to the Inn lobby and dining room, which have been restored to the character of their early days. The guest rooms have been upgraded with new finishes, and major improvements to the Inn's dated utility infrastructure have been completed. Twenty-two new, private one-bedroom casitas provide a distinct level of guest accommodations for the four-diamond property.

The newly renovated Inn lobby maintains the Inn's historic character

The new one-bedroom Casitas at the Inn

Across the highway from the Inn, using the footprint of the old commercial laundry that burned down in 2014, Xanterra Travel Collection has masterfully created the new Mission Gardens (top-next page). Using authentic California style architecture, the rehabilitated adobe walls enclose a beautifully landscaped garden area, creating the perfect venue for a wedding or any form of outdoor event. Nature provides the perfect "finish" as the nearby mountains change colors as the sunlight moves across them.

The Ranch at the Oasis at Death Valley has also seen an extensive renovation to its aging buildings and infrastructure including creation of a new mission-style town square, complete with a courtyard that elegantly welcomes guests into a streamlined, town-hall-style hotel reception area. Mission-territorial in its style, this new complex adjacent to the footprint of the original structure, includes a wrap-around porch and windows to view the square, fountain, and unique resort landscaping.

The north parking lot has been transformed into a welcoming public space, while new retail, and food and beverage facilities create a central hub for entertainment and socialization. Ranch guests now enjoy an ice cream counter, buffet, western saloon, and a new retail store with a wide variety of Death Valley souvenirs and sundries.

The new town square at the Ranch at the Oasis of Death Valley

HOT WEATHER HINTS

How to Survive Your Summer Trip Through
DEATH VALLEY

The recent and extensive renovations at both the Inn and the Ranch at the Oasis at Death Valley will help ensure this historic property continues to provide exceptional hospitality to the Death Valley visitor for years to come.

It often seems that each day, the world we live in changes at a faster and faster pace. Very little seems to stay constant in our daily lives. But the scenery and landscapes of Death Valley seem timeless. It's true that a flashflood may alter the shape of a canyon or winter rains may bring flowers where there were none before. But it's comforting to know that the serenity we find on a visit to Death Valley, will always inspire us…and bring us that same sense of fulfillment every time we return.

And in a setting so constant, lies a place that since its inception…has been providing visitors with the highest levels of extraordinary hospitality…and is still providing special fond memories that will be long remembered. This incredible National Park and the Oasis at Death Valley are magnificent places to see and visit, and as this Park Service brochure from a few years back reminds us, they will also always be…a place of the mind.

EPILOGUE

Travelers, particularly those on vacation trips, want memories they can look back on with a smile. When it comes to hotels and tourist destinations, guests expect staff members to be courteous, helpful and friendly. They also want staff members to be knowledgeable about the area and attractions. Many travelers are visiting an area for the first time and are unfamiliar with it. If staff can direct people to attractions and sites, they will help guests create those memories they crave.

Excellent customer service is vitally important in the hospitality industry. It's the first point of contact between the guest and the representative of the hotel. It is the first opportunity an establishment gets to impress and create a lasting great impression.

Great hotels and resorts know to put their customers at the forefront of their operation, and that their effort will result in a steady flow of loyal customers, that will return year after year, and even more importantly, tell others of their resplendent and memorable experience.

Since its beginning, the Oasis of Death Valley/Furnace Creek Resort has always kept the focus of its staff on providing an extraordinary and unforgettable experience that their guests will long remember. These superstars of hospitality that have worked passionately over the years, have created the foundation of the storied history of excellence that carries on as determined and dedicated as ever for their guests to enjoy today.

PHOTO CREDITS

Author's Collection, pages-2, 8, 13, 14, 15, 16, 21, 29, 33, 35 (bottom), 38, 45, 49, 52 (bottom), 58 (top & bottom), 64 (bottom), 68 bottom), 70 (top), 72 (top), 73 (bottom), 75, 77 (top & bottom), 79, 80 (bottom), 83 (top & bottom), 84 (bottom), 85 (top & bottom), 86 (top & bottom), 94-103

Photo by Burton Frasher, courtesy Rio Tinto Borax, pages-55 (top & bottom), 56 (bottom), 60, 63 (bottom), 64 (top)

Courtesy Rio Tinto Borax, pages-4, 12, 20, 23 (top), 26, 27, 28, 31, 42 (top & bottom), 43,

Photo by Burton Frasher, Eastern California Museum, pages-19, 23 (bottom), 24 (top & bottom), 25, 36, 46, 47, 51 (bottom), 65 (top & bottom), 67 (top & bottom), 73 (top)

Eastern California Museum, page-10, 11, 18, 22, 23 (top), 30, 34 (top & bottom) 35, 37, 38, 39, 40, 41 (top), 48 (top & bottom), 50, 52 (top), 53, 54 (bottom), 61, 62, 66 (top & bottom), 68 (top), 69 (top & bottom), 70 (bottom), 71 (top & bottom), 72 (bottom), 74, 76 (top & bottom), 81 (top), 87

Oregon Historical Society, page-17
Courtesy A.C. Martin Partners, Inc, pages-32
Death Valley National Park Service, page-44

Courtesy Lasley Biven, pages 51 (top), 53, 57 (bottom), 78 (top & bottom)

NY Post, page-59
Harris Shiffman, page-63 (top)

Courtesy Xanterra Travel Collection, pages-88 (top & bottom), 89, 90, 91, 92 (top & bottom), 93 (top & bottom)

Courtesy Jim Hilton, pages-81 (bottom), 82 (top & bottom)
Stock photo, page-84 (top)